BIRD DAD

A BROKEN APPLE

COPYRIGHT © EMILY BROOKS MILLAR, 2025
ISBN 978-1-0686378-3-4

BIRDDAD IS A COLLECTION OF SHORT STORIES DEPICTING THE TRIALS AND TRIBULATIONS OF BECOMING A MAN.

—

HERE LIE HIS RAMBLINGS ABOUT FLYING THE NEST, WHERE MANY FEATHERS WERE RUFFLED ALONG THE WAY...

BIRDDAD

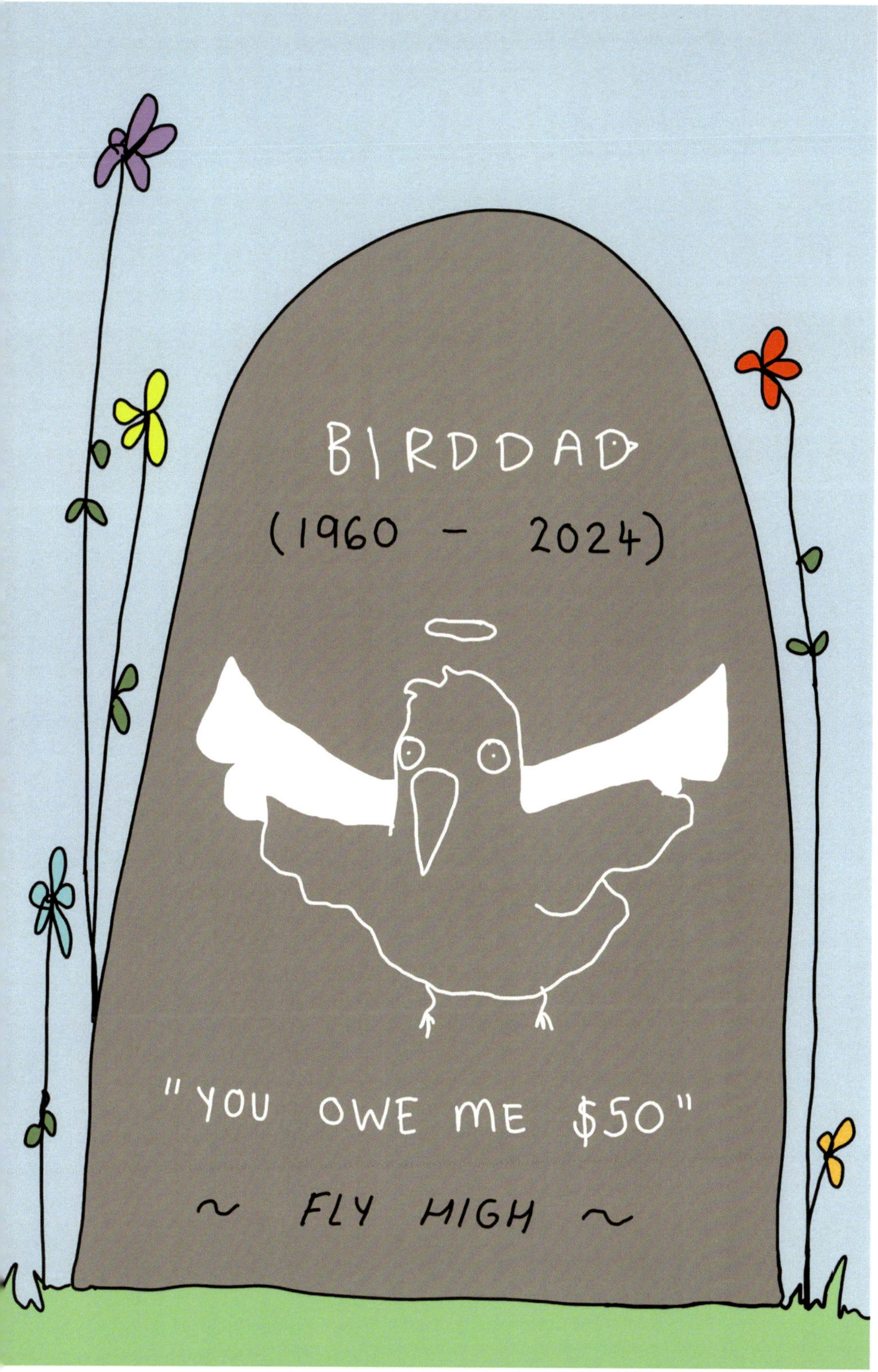
BIRDDAD
(1960 - 2024)
"YOU OWE ME $50"
~ FLY HIGH ~

1964

1973

THINGS FELL APART QUICKLY WITH MY FIRST WIFE.

I KNOW WHAT YOU DID.

WAS IT....

HE HAD MY HOME... MY KIDS...

...AND CINDY.

HE HAS BEEN MISSING FOR NEARLY 3 WEEKS.

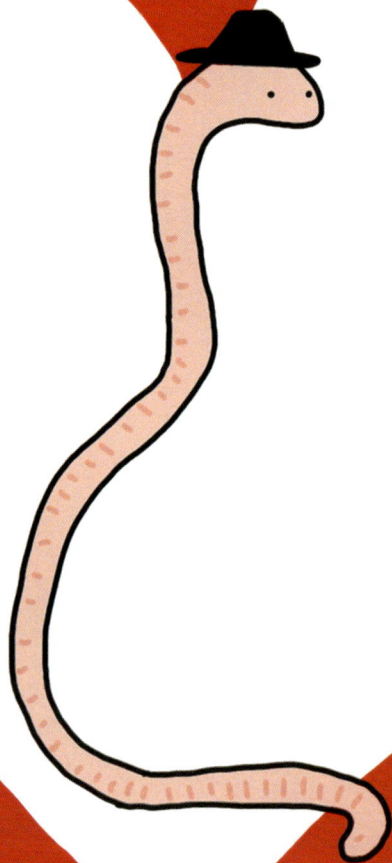

HE ALWAYS WAS A WOMANIZER

STREET DRUGS BECAME MY VICE

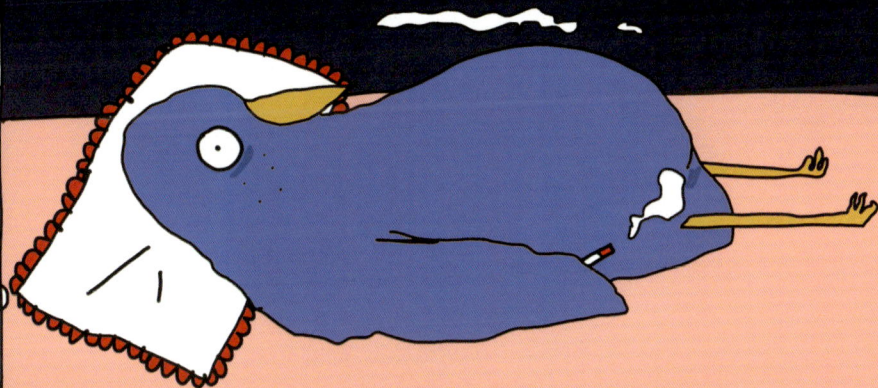

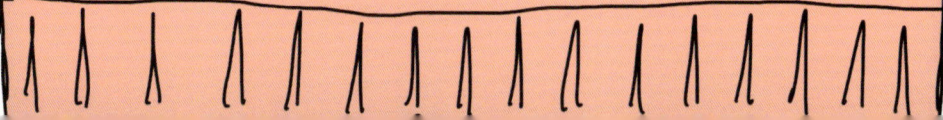

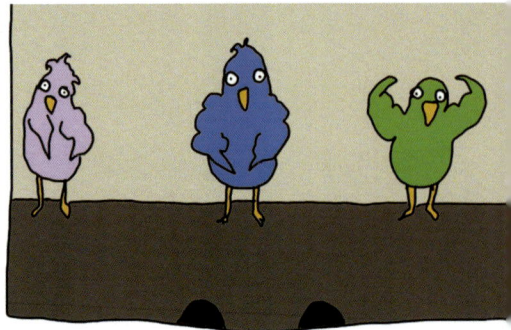

IT WAS 1989 AND I WAS A BODY BUILDING CHAMP.

IT FELT GOOD TO PROTECT THE LITTLE GUY.

BUT THEN I REALISED I COULD USE MY MUSCLES...

...FOR EVIL.

1984

1993

ALL EYES WERE ON ME

SO I RAN FOR MAYOR.

IT WAS THE BEGINNING OF MY DOWNFALL.

LET ME TELL YOU ABOUT THE TIME I WAS A BIG MOVIE PRODUCER.

FAST CARS

ACTRESSES

A THICK MATTRESS

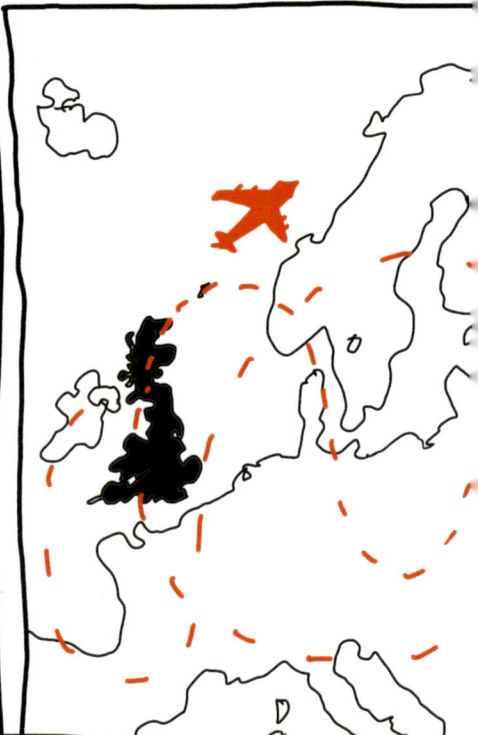

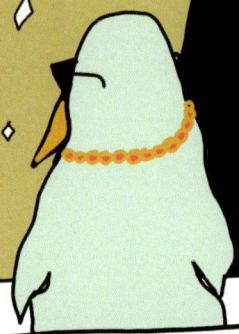

BIRDGER

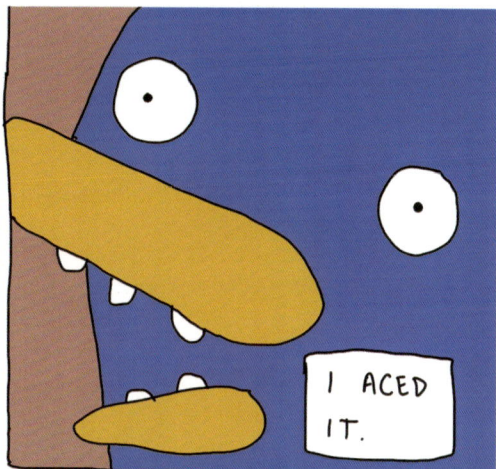

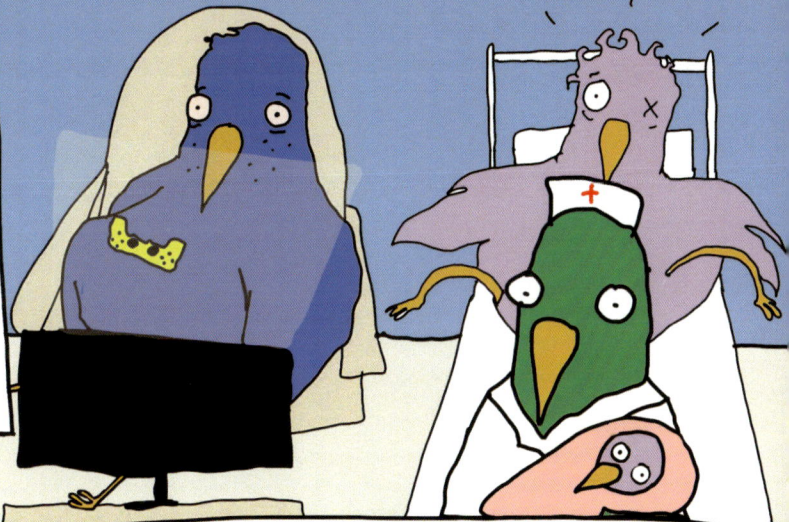

I WAS ON MY THIRD DAY OF SURVEILLANCE

WHEN MY BATTERY RAN LOW.

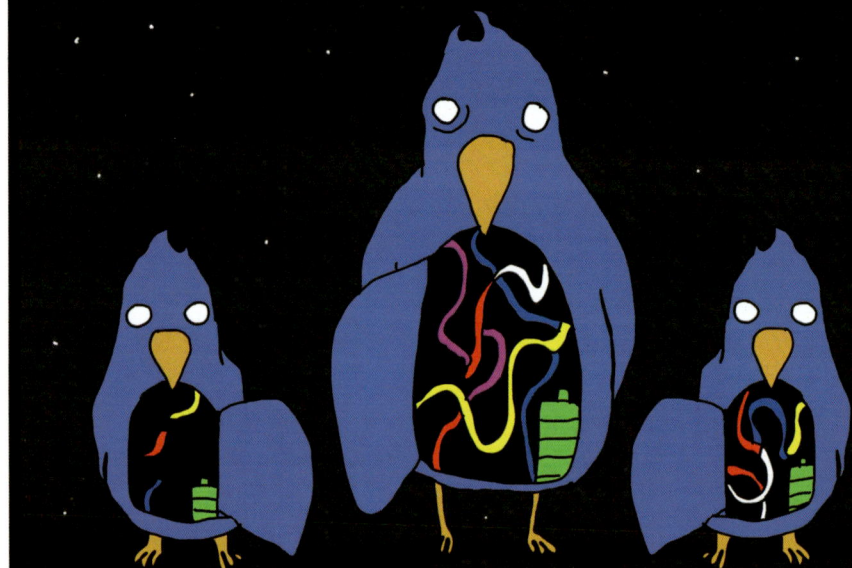

NURTURE

PROVIDE

INSPIRE

CONQUER

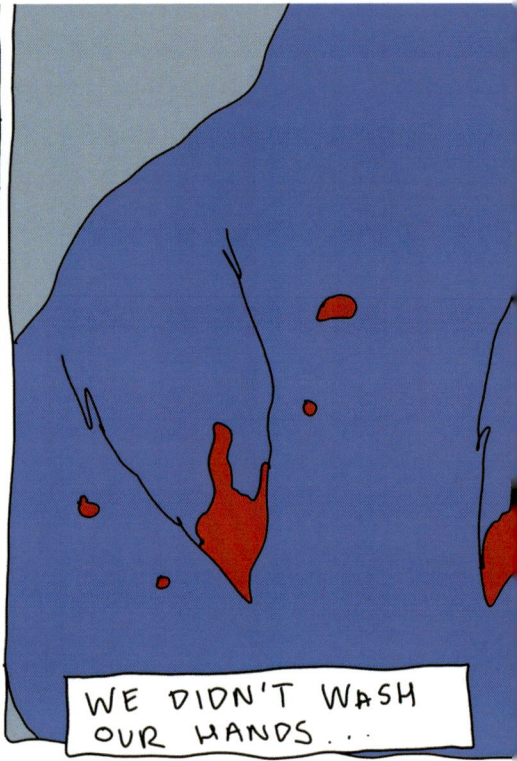

I ALWAYS ACE IT.

I HAVE ALWAYS BEEN THE ALPHA

IT'S FAMILY GROCERY DAY!

LIST

JUST ME AND MY BOYS

FOOD

MY SONS ARE STARS!

AND NOW THEY'RE SUING ME...

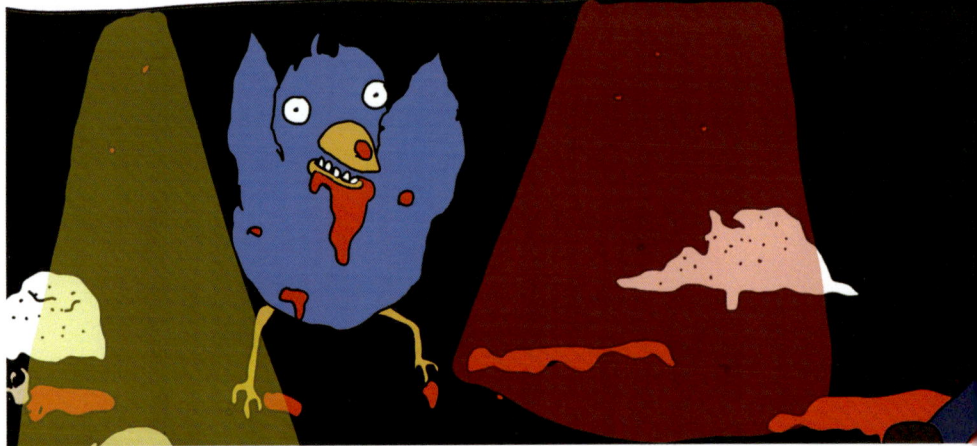

THIS SPRING CHICKEN NEEDS TO KEEP IT FRESH.

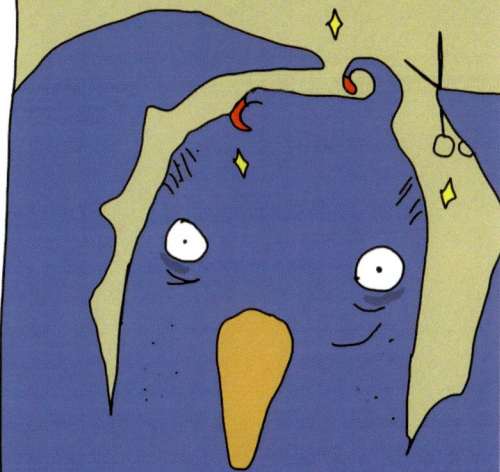

NEW 'DO

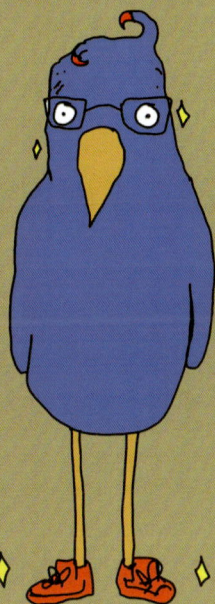

NEW KICKS

PIZZAZZ

HOT DADS DRINK BEER AND PLAY FOOTBALL

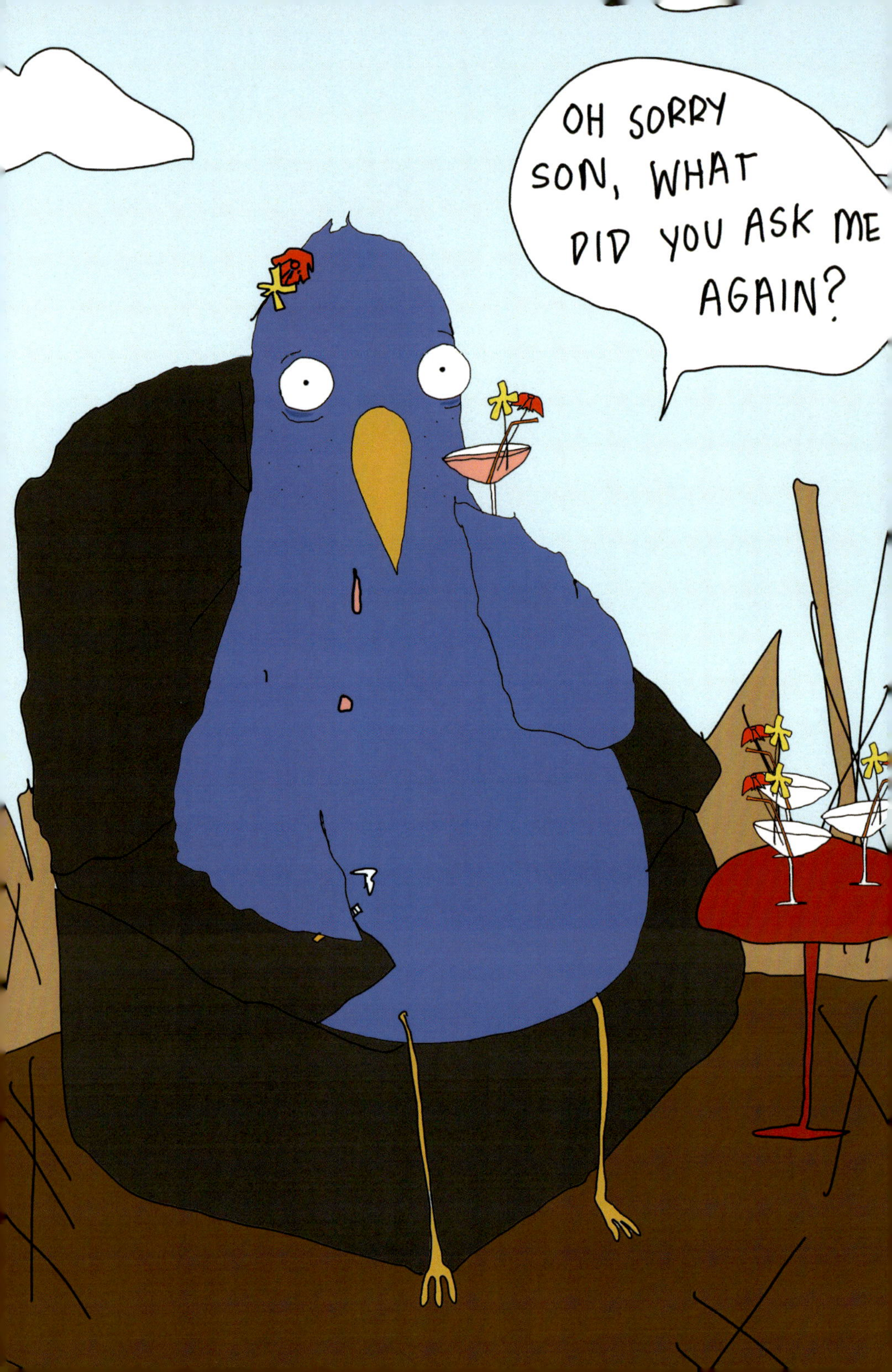
OH SORRY SON, WHAT DID YOU ASK ME AGAIN?

BIRDDAD   CINDY

GRAVEL #2 TINY

WORM

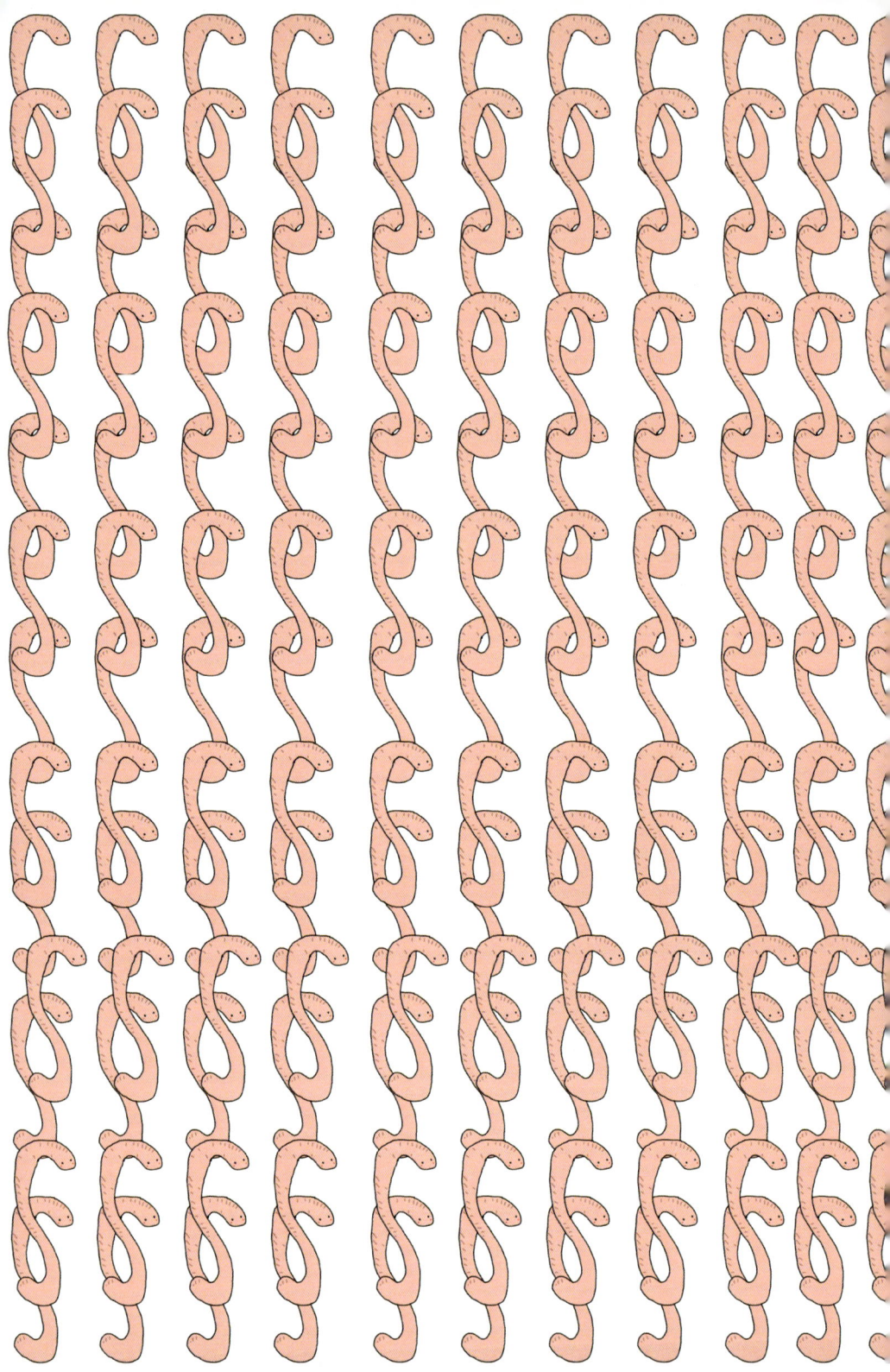

(ABOUT THE CREATOR)

EMILY BROOKS MILLAR IS AN AUTHOR & VISUAL ARTIST FROM SCOTLAND. SHE HAS ILLUSTRATED FOR GROUPS SUCH AS IMAGE COMICS, BBC & THE BIG ISSUE. HER PAINTING COLLECTIONS EXHIBIT INTERNATIONALLY AND CAN BE FOUND AT:

EMILYBROOKSMILLAR.COM

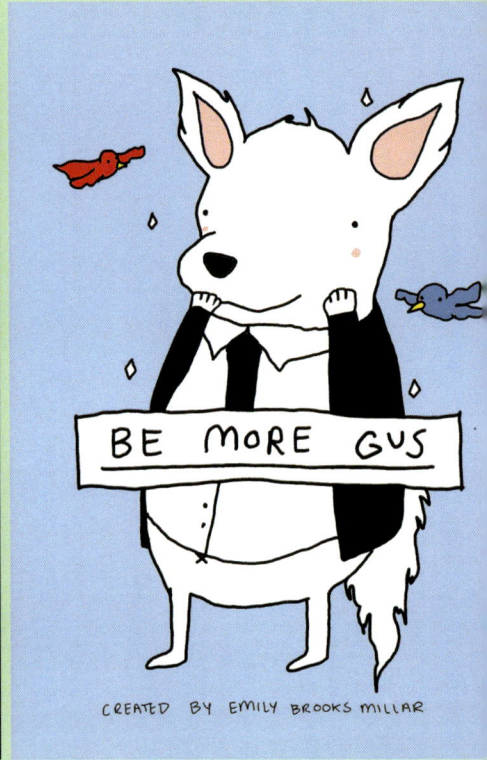